Derek,
Dublin's Gentle Giant

HELEN MACBROOM

ATHENA PRESS
LONDON

DEREK, DUBLIN'S GENTLE GIANT
Copyright © Helen MacBroom 2008

ISBN: 978 1 84748 251 8

First Published 2008 by
ATHENA PRESS
Queen's House, 2 Holly Road
Twickenham TW1 4EG
United Kingdom

Printed for Athena Press

Acknowledgements

I would like to express my gratitude and thanks to the following people:

My parents, Bob and Elsie Howe, who brought Derek and me into this great adventure.

My dear husband, Stan MacBroom, who became a true, caring brother to Derek.

My daughter, Fiona MacBroom, who spent many hours typing the original manuscript.

My daughter, Jennifer MacBroom, who always remembered to visit Derek.

My son, Michael MacBroom, who never tired of hearing Derek's funny stories and who wants to see the story in a film.

Councillor Mary Freehill, who helped Derek find a secure home.

Grace Maguire and Gerry Barry from Dublin City Council, who showed true friendship to Derek and me.

Mary Brennan and Rosin, the wardens at Maxwell Court, who kept an eye on Derek.

Reverend Alan and Ruth Boal, Neill and Cilla Fitzell, Robert Poynton and everyone at Abbey Church.

All Derek's former workmates from the Parks Department Depot.

Red Hurley, who inspired and befriended Derek.

The Irish artist who drew Derek's portrait.

Jenny from the Kingfisher.

Dr Peter Staunton and Dr Ciara O'Shea.

Last, but of most importance, all the neighbours in Maxwell Court in Rathmines.

You all played important parts in Derek's unique life.

*Dedicated to the people of Dublin
who showed friendship and kindness
to Derek and to everyone out there
who lives with Asperger's Syndrome*

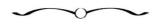

Derek as a baby, 1940

Chapter One
The Early Years

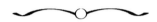

O N THE 9TH SEPTEMBER 1939, my brother Derek was born to Elsie and Bob Howe. He was their firstborn child and longed-for son.

Derek was a beautiful, perfectly formed baby, and my parents were delighted with him. During his babyhood, my mother devoted herself to caring for him, and with his bright smiley face and jolly personality, he brought them much joy.

Sadly, for everyone alive at that period in history, World War II was declared that same week.

Mum, Dad and Derek lived in a small, rented terrace house in the heart of east Belfast. The house was close to Harland & Wolff Shipyard which was to become a target for the German bombers on their nightly air raids over Belfast.

They used to hide under the stairs to feel safer. Mum stuffed Derek's ears with cotton wool to try and deaden the noise a little but the wail of the sirens and the dull sickening thud of the bombs could still be heard. Little Derek was so frightened he screamed and cried, and there was no way they could pacify him. This way of trying to cope with the dire situation was obviously not working for them, so, like most of the people in east Belfast, every night the little family made their way on foot to the relative safety of the Castlereagh hills. There the people sat or lay down under the trees and hedgerows where they heard the bombs from a safe distance. When dawn broke, they all wearily made their way back on foot to their homes – that is, if their homes were still standing.

One night, Tower Street, close to where Mum and Dad lived, took a direct hit and everyone in the street was killed. Dad cycled round that morning to see if there was anything he could do, but the scene of utter devastation overwhelmed him so much he then decided that they were no longer safe living in Belfast. Dad began looking for a safe place in the country.

By now the Belfast children were being evacuated to the country anyway, but Derek, being an infant, was far too young to be separated from Mammy.

At last Dad found a place named Ballyalton House, in the countryside outside Newtownards. There they would be safe. Derek absolutely loved the countryside, where he played peacefully, in safety, amongst the trees and hedgerows. There were other young children living there and Derek enjoyed their company. He thrived in this natural environment.

In May 1945 the war was finally over. Derek was now six years old and doing really well. Dad got a job as a painter and decorator, which came with a rented terrace house in the suburbs of south Belfast. The family moved there for new beginnings, hoping for peace and security.

The night the war ended everyone celebrated. Mum and Dad went in to Belfast city centre. It seemed that the whole world was having a party. People were singing and dancing in the streets. They were dancing in circles around the Albert Clock, kissing and embracing. Life promised to be good once more.

In February 1946, nine months after these riotous celebrations, there was a baby boom. I was part of that scene, and arrived in to this world on 13 February 1946. My destiny, among many things, was to be Derek's sister and only sibling.

I loved growing up in Stranmillis. The area was tree-lined, quiet and peaceful. At that time poverty was rife – there were food and clothing shortages. Everyone was issued

The wall at Ballyalton, 1942,
a safe haven for Derek

with a ration book, and people had to spend hours queuing for basic necessities.

As a young child, I was blissfully unaware of this. Everyone I knew had few possessions. I played with old ration books, out-of-date paint cards and wallpaper trimmings. Using imagination, it's amazing what fun children can have without games or toys.

Derek was in my life from the day I was born. He was the big brother who loved me and helped care for me. He played with me and made me feel really special. Derek shared all his rations with me and would not even take a sweet until he made sure I had a sweet too.

As we grew older and played outside, if anyone bullied me or gave me any sort of trouble, I simply told Derek, who promptly went to the culprit and 'sorted them out'. I adored Derek, as did Mum and Dad.

When Derek started the local primary school he did remarkably well. He learned to read and write quickly and numbers seemed to be his speciality. He was also talented musically, having a good singing voice and learning to play the piano and read music. Our maternal grandfather was Tom Stevenson, a well-known professional musician in

Belfast. Tom sang opera, played the piano and violin, and also taught music and singing. Tom gave many a concert in the Ulster Hall in Belfast, where Elsie, our mother, would accompany him on the piano, being a talented singer and pianist herself. Music was obviously in Derek's genes, so he was bought a piano. Derek showed such promise in those early years that my parents had high hopes for his future.

We were a happy family. Dad by now was running his own thriving painting and decorating business. In his spare time he painted pictures and indulged in his passion for astronomy. Dad owned a large heavy telescope, which took two strong men to lift. The telescope rested on large red trestles. This sat at our front window on the first floor of our Stranmillis terrace, and on clear evenings we were shown the moon, with all its craters and mountains, and the many other beautiful planets and stars within our solar system. Our favourite planet was Saturn, with its beautifully coloured spinning rings. When the evenings were warm and particularly clear, Dad used to get help to take his telescope, complete with trestles, out on to the Stranmillis Road where a large queue of people quickly formed. There was little in the way of entertainment in the 1950s, so queuing in the street to have a look through Dad's telescope was an exciting thing to do. Everyone was amazed at the beauty and perfect order of the planets and stars. These activities had a profound effect on Derek, who loved being close to our natural world.

Our home was filled with good books, all the classics and books of a philosophical and spiritual nature. A love of reading was instilled in both Derek and me by Mum.

Derek had a great love for animals, and so did I. Mum taught us to always show kindness and compassion to all 'dumb animals', as she put it. To Derek and me, none of the animals were dumb because we could communicate with them really well.

Every stray dog and cat in the neighbourhood found a safe haven in our home. We also had rabbits, and our bath was often filled with frogspawn which Derek had carefully collected in empty jam pots from the local River Lagan. This, of course, meant that our bathroom was frequently filled with frogs of various shapes and sizes hopping around. When it all got too much in our tiny bathroom, Dad made Derek gather them all up in a bucket and take them back to the Lagan.

Derek was always wandering away and had to be looked

for. This was a major problem for my parents. He could usually be found in Botanic Gardens among the trees he loved, or else down at the River Lagan.

On one particular occasion Derek was in neither of these favourite haunts of his. When time wore on to 10.30 p.m. my parents began to panic and alerted the police who immediately began a search for him. Later that evening, a large country bus drove up the Stranmillis Road, stopped at our front door and Derek and his little dog climbed out. Apparently the driver had been doing a late shift and spotted Derek and the dog miles away, walking along a country road, and thought something was wrong. He brought Derek and the dog safely back home, and everyone was relieved. From that day on Derek was kept locked in his little back-attic bedroom after school. Dad boarded his window with strips of plywood in order to keep him safe.

The attic then became Derek's refuge and hiding place from the world. As time went on and we were growing up, I noticed all the local children laughing at Derek and taunting him. It was really unpleasant. Why were they treating him in this way? Physically he was much bigger and stronger than any of them, but he also seemed 'different'. Because he was my brother I could not understand the reason for it.

At around this time Derek's school work began to suffer. He was often found daydreaming and looking out of the window. His teachers could not get him to pay attention. Dad blamed the teachers' poor teaching skills and promptly took him away from the school. The next week Derek was sent off to a different school where the same pattern repeated itself. He was at more schools in Belfast than anyone I ever knew. Bear in mind that in those early post-war years there was neither knowledge nor help available for either gifted children or children with special needs. Most teachers were armed with a cane and you tried to fit in as much as possible. Derek, being misunderstood, was caned frequently. It was a case of sink or swim, and Derek was sinking fast.

He was so unhappy by this time that he used to escape from school and run home crying and screaming, often from schools on the other side of Belfast. I found this extremely distressing and no one seemed to know what to do.

In summer, Derek took refuge playing amongst the trees, or, in winter, locked in his tiny back-room attic. I just played around the streets, as children do, with a vague unease that all was definitely not well.

In those less enlightened days, any mental or physical disability had a huge stigma attached to it. If Derek was kept away in the attic then maybe nobody would realise he wasn't coping. Indeed, that was to be his fate.

In the early 1960s some of our American relations came to stay for a holiday. Derek appeared briefly to literally say hello, then went straight back to his attic. Word got around that the boy was 'odd'.

It hurt me deeply to hear people talking and laughing about him, especially when it was coming from my friends. I observed all these things going on and knew there was nothing I could do to make the situation any better for him.

CHAPTER TWO
ADOLESCENCE AND YOUNG ADULTHOOD

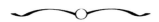

I N THE SIXTIES things were improving and people were generally more prosperous. Work was readily available in many areas of Belfast and, for the first time in history, home ownership was a possibility for ordinary working people.

The music scene was exciting. Dance halls were opening up everywhere, and the general atmosphere was optimistic and positive. The Beatles went to India, and yoga and meditation came to the west. Derek loved both traditional Irish music and The Beatles so, between the two of us, we had a great collection of music.

Fashion was youthful, colourful and fun, and we had good times with our many relatives and friends coming and going.

School days were over, thankfully, and as work was plentiful in our area we both found jobs. At this time our parents rented a lovely traditional whitewashed cottage in Ravensdale, just outside Dundalk. We spent many weekends there and most of our holidays, even in winter time. Ravensdale was an exceptionally beautiful place. Our cottage had only one living room and two bedrooms. Mum, Dad and I had one room, and Derek and our dog had the other. We cooked on an open fire and led a simple, carefree life there.

Local shopping trips were to Dundalk, where we picked up many a bargain in the old antique shops to help furnish our wee cottage.

The local people of Ravensdale were extremely warm and friendly. Derek and I simply dropped in to their cottages to visit and they always made us welcome. Derek seemed to fit in there and thoroughly enjoyed it all. Being in Ravensdale was a sharp contrast to his experiences growing up in Belfast.

Trips to Dublin were frequent. We loved Dublin. During the 1950s, after the war, we often travelled to Dundalk, and sometimes to Dublin, to bring back food and clothes. We would smuggle these extras in the cardboard picnic box which was kept in our car boot.

The Irish customs officers used to wave to us and smile, and we got through easily, but the British customs officers were quite different. Sometimes they would look in to the car and let us drive through, but more often than not we would be ordered out of the car and made to stand at the side of the road while they stripped the car and boot in search of possible extra food or anything else from the Republic.

On one particular occasion, Dad had made me a dolls' house for my birthday. Due to the rationing the little house had no furniture, so on our next trip to Dublin Dad found a little table and chairs and some tiny dolls to put in to the house. He hid them carefully at the bottom of the picnic box, covered them up with old papers, then put the picnic things on top.

When we got to the Irish Customs Office there was no problem, as usual, but as we drove slowly towards the British Customs Office I began to feel quite nervous. Would they wave us through, or would we be searched this time? To my horror, we were ordered to stand out by the side of the road while the searching began. Nothing was found inside the car, but then the officer ordered Dad to open the boot. When he began going through the picnic box, my heart sank and I felt panic rising within myself; I desperately wanted to fill my dolls' house with people and furniture. He lifted out the food and removed the papers, and there at the bottom of the box were my precious little dolls. As he held up the tiny pieces of furniture and examined them I felt all was lost. I had nothing to lose, so I began to cry and scream, flinging myself on the ground. Dad said, 'Mister, have you no children of your own? Have some pity.' The officer paused for a moment, obviously feeling a bit sorry for us, stuffed the toys back in the box and let us through. The scene I created had worked. Looking back on this now, I have to laugh. We were just an ordinary family with little money, like most people living there at that time. Was he hoping to find diamonds?

These events had a profound effect on Derek, who saw the Irish as the 'Goodies' and the British as the 'Baddies'.

With rationing now long gone, we no longer needed to smuggle anything over the border, and our trips to Dublin were pure pleasure. We admired the architecture and beautifully made Georgian doors. Dublin had amazing art galleries and lots of cultural activities.

Derek always felt Dublin was his home, as his experiences there had only been good. At twenty-three years old he decided to spend the rest of his life there, as he had never fitted in to the neighbourhood in Belfast. Derek saved all his earnings and, in the summer of 1962, left Belfast, and our home, for ever. He said he would go there and find work and a place to live. He was incredibly brave, but our parents, relations and neighbours told him he was very foolish as he could never make it in Dublin: he knew no one and had no contacts there to help him. Derek's determination was great however, and he set off for Dublin for good.

Mum and Dad said it must be in his genes, as our great-grandparents were from Tipperary and, as a young couple, were lucky enough to flee the famine and make their way to Lisburn, County Antrim, where our great-grandfather found work. They rented a terrace house in an area known as the Long Stone. The house had a long narrow back garden which enabled them to grow vegetables. They had escaped the starvation and certain death which was to be the fate of the rest of our ancestors living in the surrounding areas of Tipperary and Skibereen at that time.

Later, our great-grandmother brought up Dad herself; he was the eldest child of a large family, and she took him on to give our grandmother more time to devote to the younger brothers and sisters.

Dad loved living with this interesting lady. She spoke with a beautiful soft brogue and encouraged him in his love of art. It was from her that Dad learned a lot about Irish history. He used to tell us many of her stories, and this probably helped to influence Derek in his love for Ireland.

Derek returned to Belfast for the occasional day trip only, but he frequently met us at Ravensdale where we would spend weekends and holidays together. We often went to Dublin to visit him and make sure he was coping all right.

Those early days in Dublin were a terrible struggle for Derek. He had little money and knew absolutely no one. Every morning he would get up early and tramp the streets asking for work. He offered to do just about anything. He tried every shop and factory in the city, from Brown Thomas (who chased him away) to individuals living in big houses, where he offered to do their gardens. Derek was a strong, healthy young man and was capable of any sort of physical work. Thankfully some people did let him work in their gardens, digging, planting and tidying up the leaves in autumn. He worked hard and was trustworthy, therefore most people asked him to work for them on a regular basis. Occasionally he was given a meal, which was an added bonus. Life for Derek improved, and his needs were simple.

In those early weeks in Dublin, Derek rented a room on the north side of Dublin's inner city. He managed to get factory work there but, sadly, as always, he did not fit in with the other workers. Derek was 'different', which made many people feel a little uncomfortable.

He was attacked and beaten up several times, and had no idea why. In Derek's mind the attackers were just the Baddies, and Derek knew that he was definitely one of the Goodies, and that was the end of the matter. Once, some local lads set their vicious dogs on him. Fortunately Derek was strong and healthy enough to survive the attack. He managed to escape with just a few bite wounds. Derek had an affinity with all animals and did not blame the dogs, just the Baddies who had trained them in this way.

By far the most serious attack was one winter evening as Derek was making his way home from work; he was chased by a ruthless gang and this time they managed to catch him and hold him down. He was outnumbered and unable to get away. They set fire to his clothes and ran away laughing. Fortunately Derek had the good sense to roll himself on the ground to put the flames out. This incident really shook him up and he came back to Belfast to tell us about it. Derek could not report these incidents to the Garda, as he would have had no idea how to go about it. We pleaded with him to stay with us so we could look after him, but he knew he did not fit in anywhere in Belfast, and said he would leave that place in Dublin where the Baddies lived and try his luck on the south side of Dublin over the River Liffey.

Chapter Three
Derek's Heydays

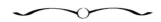

B Y NOW THE swinging sixties were well underway. Dance halls were opening up everywhere. The music scene was fantastic, and there was a general air of new-found freedom in society.

Derek had grown in to an exceptionally handsome young man. He had film-star looks. He was over six feet tall with tanned skin, due to so much time spent in the open air. His eyes were clear blue and he had thick dark hair. With his gentle manners and friendly personality, Derek could win anyone over with his Irish charm.

Derek did try his luck on the south side of Dublin as he intended. With his regular work as a gardener he earned enough money to pay rent in shared accommodation. During this period he was befriended by students from Trinity College, and his life improved living in the Rathmines area of south Dublin. At last Derek fitted in somewhere. He was accepted by the people who got to know him. To the well-educated young men from Trinity, being 'different' was quite acceptable. In fact, being 'different' made one appear more interesting. Red Hurley, the famous Irish singer and entertainer, also befriended Derek. Red often dedicated some of his songs to Derek, and Derek was so proud of this. He even brought Red to visit our family in Belfast and have a meal with Mum. Mum kept a signed picture of Red on her fireplace, and was delighted that at last Derek had found people to share part of his life with. Derek was asked to many parties and was a hit with some of the girls.

Life improved even more for Derek when he got permanent employment with Dublin Corporation, now known as Dublin City Council. At last we could relax knowing Derek would have a regular pay cheque and, if he reached pension age, would retire with a reasonable pension.

On our holidays to Dublin, Derek would take me out to various dance halls in the city, where I had a great time dancing the night away. I felt totally safe as Derek just dutifully stood at the back of the hall watching over me. He never complained about doing this, rather he seemed to enjoy it. When the dances were over, Derek would walk back with me to wherever we were staying, and after seeing me in safely, would then walk back to his own place in Rathmines.

Derek's job with the council was to check all the parking meters on the streets of Dublin to see if any needed repairing and also to keep them clean. He would take down the number of any broken meter and the name of the street and report this back to the office. This was ideal work for Derek. With his need for the open air and his love of people and numbers, he had at long last found his niche in life. Derek had an amazing photographic memory and soon got to know every street in Dublin. He talked to everyone, and if anyone appeared lost, Derek would go to them and give them directions – he did not need a map. He was fast becoming a bit of a celebrity on the streets of Dublin. Just about everyone knew him. With his larger-than-life frame and his now long, reddish dark beard and exceptionally friendly personality, people wondered who this big fellow was and where he came from.

Derek gave many interviews for local newspapers and magazines. He was interviewed by a famous television personality and journalist, the late Russell Harty, and appeared in a photograph with Russell in one of the glossy

A dream come true working on the streets of Dublin

magazines. Local radio stations interviewed him and he appeared on television. Derek won a competition called 'Know Your Dublin'. Nobody knew Dublin better than Derek.

Derek being interviewed by the late Russell Harty

Derek was photographed by many foreign tourists and also appeared on an Irish calendar called Faces of Ireland.

A famous Irish artist drew his portrait. Derek used to go to the artist's home and sit for him professionally. His portrait hung in Fairview Art Gallery for a while; he proudly brought us to see it. I wish I had had the means to buy it, but in those days it would not have been possible. Someone, somewhere, has it, and it is a perfect likeness of Derek in his heyday.

Our family trips to Dublin were more enjoyable than ever now; wherever we went everybody knew our Derek. Mum and Dad were so happy to see how successful his life had become and could now rest easy. Derek had been accepted in society and had made it.

CHAPTER FOUR
MORE CHANGES

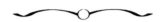

ROUND THIS TIME, our dad was in his fifties and decided he had done enough physical work. He applied for a job as a paint consultant and, fortunately, got it. The job was based both in Belfast and in Dublin. Dad would work for two weeks in Belfast and two weeks in Dublin.

One of the perks of the job was a luxury apartment in Dublin city centre. This meant that Derek could move out of his student-style accommodation and live in luxury at Dad's flat.

Derek had the qualities of total innocence and purity. He was like a child who had never grown up, and, in truth, he never had grown up. Inside that large man's body was a pure soul who was vulnerable and needed to be cared for.

It was now the late 1960s and life was changing as always. We received a letter telling us we could no longer rent the cottage at Ravensdale as it was to be used for other purposes.

Our family was really disappointed on hearing this news, as Ravensdale had become not only our holiday home but our halfway house where we could easily meet up with Derek.

In the summer of 1969 the troubles came to Northern Ireland and life changed unbelievably: for the worse. I had just married Stan that summer and we had begun setting up home in Lisburn. By strange coincidence this was very near the place where my great-grandparents had fled many years before, in search of a refuge from the famine which ravaged most of Ireland at that time. We had chosen Lisburn simply because the houses were cheaper than in Belfast. Everyone was depressed and the air of joy and vibrant buzz of Belfast seemed to evaporate overnight. What did the future hold for us? Many people simply emigrated to escape whatever was to come. Having been born after the war, I had absolutely no concept of bombings and shootings. Lisburn was particularly badly hit; we frequently had to run out of shops and were unsure in which direction to escape. Everyone suffered in one way or another, and often life felt unbearable.

When our first child was born we decided it would be better to move to a safer area of Belfast, and fortunately we lived relatively peacefully there. During the 1970s we had two more babies and I stayed at home to look after them. Staying at home was the safest way to live. The children were too young to know anything about the situation.

During these difficult years Derek was continuing to thrive and was enjoying living his dream on the streets of Dublin. We were all really happy for him, and thankful that at least he was safe there. Derek and I wrote to each other frequently, as he was always a great letter-writer. He was afraid to come to the north, and I would not leave my babies to go to Dublin.

Dad's job as a paint consultant came to an end. With the loss of his job came the loss of the luxury flat in Dublin. This meant that Dad came back to live in Belfast full-time, and Derek found himself, yet again, alone on the streets of Dublin.

By now several years had passed. All Derek's former flat-mates had found good jobs, married and had homes and families of their own. Derek had nobody – but at least he was a well-known street character in Dublin city centre.

Derek found himself walking the streets of Dublin looking for accommodation. In his innocence, he fell prey to many unscrupulous landlords who exploited him, charging him exorbitant rent for tiny basement rooms with poor facilities. Derek seemed to be unaware of this and, in his innocence, simply accepted the situation and paid up. He even bought toys for some of his landlords' children, which, of course, were accepted.

We were now living in the 1980s, and my children were growing up and settling in to school life. I longed to see Derek again, and although we had always been in touch, I needed to go and see him in person to find out how he really was. When I saw him in his rented room in Dublin I was shocked and appalled at his squalid living conditions. I was used to seeing him with his former friends or in Dad's luxury flat. Now that he was really on his own it was quite obvious to me that he was not coping well. How could this have happened? Did anyone but me know or care about his plight?

Mum and Dad advised me not to worry about him so much, as Derek was a born survivor. He had managed alone in Dublin all these years and they felt confident he would be all right.

I could not stop worrying about him though. I felt power-less to help him as my life was in Belfast with my family and my part-time work. Indeed, I worried so much that my own health broke. Derek remained oblivious to his situation and his happy letters to us continued. Derek was enjoying life – this time it was me going under.

The main concern I had was what would become of him when he retired. He would not be able to afford the rents he was being charged and could end up living rough on the streets. No one would know the reality of his situation, only me.

The one positive aspect was that time was on his side. Derek intended to work until he was sixty-six, which was many years away. Derek was so happy living his dream on the streets of Dublin that nothing else mattered to him.

I decided it was important to spend more time with him and try to understand him better. Later on I would do my utmost to find him a safe, affordable place to live.

Our parents were bombed out of their home twice, due to it being beside a large hotel which had become a target for the bombers. They, along with their neighbours, had to take shelter in a local hospital room for safety during the night. We lived on the other side of Belfast which meant we were unable to travel over until daytime. Everyone felt safer simply staying in their own areas.

On one occasion, when Dad was with Derek in Dublin, there was an almighty bang and a dull thud which sounded just like a bomb exploding. Surely these things only happened in the north? Next morning they discovered that

Nelson's Pillar, a large monument in O'Connell Street, had been blown up. Later on that evening, there was a loud knock at Derek's door. Derek opened it to find several Garda had come to question him about the incident. Poor Derek was shocked – he was incapable of doing such a thing. We knew this, but the Garda did not. As luck would have it, Dad was there, and he stepped forward to assure them that Derek was indeed in the flat with him when the event took place.

If Dad had not been with Derek at that time, I shudder to think what could have happened. Derek may well have been taken in to custody and asked to sign a confession. Knowing Derek, he would have signed anything he was asked to. It seems that Derek had been seen handing out leaflets on the streets of Dublin. This had aroused the suspicion of the Garda, who began watching his activities. If Derek had been asked to hand out leaflets by anyone, he would have agreed, because that was his nature – he would help anyone in any way he could.

We were relieved that Dad had been there, and hoped Derek would not be in a similar situation again. Fortunately he never was.

CHAPTER FIVE
RITUALS, OBSESSIONS AND
EXTRAORDINARY ABILITIES

NOW THAT MY children were older, I had more time to spend with Derek, getting to know him as an adult and trying to understand his complex personality and funny ways. People had got used to the troubles by now and could usually gauge when it felt safe to travel.

Derek began travelling to Belfast again on any free day he had off work, and always on his birthday. I listened carefully to him and soon got to understand him better, or at least *tried* to. Spending time with Derek was never dull or boring – he always made me laugh. Derek was direct and completely honest in his speech. He spoke from his heart. If you did not like what he said then it was your problem, not his. I found his childlike simplicity and light-hearted outlook on life, with all its problems, quite refreshing compared with other people's attitudes.

Generosity was one of Derek's characteristics. Every time he visited us he was laden with presents for the children – dolls and good quality toy cars. He also brought lots of food, so as not to use up all of mine. One of his specialities was large bars of white chocolate, so that the children would not make a mess. Our children loved this large, gentle uncle who played with them at their own level. He spent endless time talking and listening to them.

By now I was aware that Derek had several obsessions. One was the colour green, which he talked about a lot throughout our conversations. His letters to me usually mentioned 'green', and the colour 'green' was always written in green ink. He also liked the numbers nine, eleven and fifteen. Whatever story he was telling us, one of these three numbers would feature in it.

Derek repeated the same stories over and over again. We got to know them off by heart. Perhaps when he saw us all falling about laughing at these stories it encouraged him to keep telling them. One of his favourite stories, and ours, was about the password for getting past a goose. We would all be sitting round the table having a meal when Derek would say, 'I know the secret password for getting past a goose.' He would then wait for our reaction.

'What is it, Derek? Go on, tell us the secret password!'

'It's easy,' he said. 'You just walk up to it, hold out your hand and say "Tweet Tweet Tweet", then it lets you walk past.'

We would all be in kinks with laughter, and he laughed too. We had to wonder just how often he encountered a fierce goose while working on the streets of Dublin. It was only a few days after Derek died that the real reason for his obsession with the password story came back to me.

Many years before, in the 1950s, long before our Ravensdale days, Dad used to rent a little wooden hut situated beside the sea at Ballintoy Harbour on the Antrim Coast. Our family and friends loved that place. It was, and still is, an area of outstanding natural beauty. The summers in the 1950s were long and hot, and although we had absolutely no facilities in the hut, we thrived on fresh sea air and sunshine.

There were no shops, so a mobile grocery van used to drive round a few times each week, always at around 3 a.m. (the middle of the night to most people). The driver would honk his horn loudly to wake us up, and Mum would go out with a torch and a basket to buy enough basic provisions to keep us going until his next nightly visit. There were only four or five people living there full-time: a lovely lady and her husband called Mr and Mrs O'Rourke, and two elderly fishermen who lived in the cottage next door. Mrs O'Rourke used to bake the most delicious scones, and during the summer months would set tables and chairs outside her cottage and sell tea and scones to the day trippers. We called at her cottage every day, and Derek especially enjoyed the craic of the two fishermen when he visited them. Getting drinking water was a different matter. The grocery van and Mrs O'Rourke ensured that there was always enough to eat, but the only way to get water was to draw it from a well in the large cave near the cottages.

Derek was always big and strong, so each morning Mum gave him two large buckets and Derek's job was to draw the water from the well and carry it back to the hut. I used to run with him to keep him company. Every time we reached the stone wall outside the cottages, a gaggle of geese that obviously lived there would rise up, flap their strong wings, then lower their bodies to the ground and run at us, squawking loudly and pecking at our heels. We never wore socks in summertime, so it was not a pleasant experience. Other children who were holidaying there often came with us and we noticed that none of the geese ever pecked Derek, only the rest of us. I would stand directly behind him, and race past with him in the front line to try and avoid getting my heels pecked.

'I know their secret password,' he would say proudly. 'That's why they let me past.' He refused to divulge it to us and, being children, this was a great mystery, and no doubt gave Derek a sense of importance. It is only now that on thinking back to these hilarious occasions I realise it was simply because Derek was carrying the large buckets that the geese were afraid to peck at him.

To this very day, every morning, if anyone wants to get in to our bathroom, we always tap the door and shout 'Tweet Tweet Tweet'. It has become a standard joke, like many of Derek's sayings.

Cards were another of Derek's obsessions. Derek never forgot anyone's birthday. His cards always arrived exactly two weeks in advance of the date. On opening his card, you would always find that he had written, on the line below the message: 'I am sending this card early in case of a postal strike.' This pattern of sending our birthday cards two weeks in advance was carried on right until he died.

Whenever Derek went on holiday, or even on a day trip, he would send everyone he knew postcards, every day, and in abundance. Cards were of the utmost importance to him.

Alarm clocks were another of Derek's obsessions. He would carry between six and eight small travel alarm clocks around with him, one for each pocket. Trouser pockets, shirt pockets, jacket pockets and overcoat pockets all housed a travel alarm clock. He set these clocks regularly and they were forever going off. This was especially funny whenever we took him to a posh restaurant or café. We would all be sitting round the table when, suddenly, an alarm clock would go off. Everyone was definitely looking our way! Derek would stop everything, look up, and listen to hear exactly from which pocket the sound was coming. He would then fish out the clock, stop the alarm and promptly reset it again. This ritual gave him a lot of pleasure. A little while later, another alarm clock would go off, and the whole ritual would begin again. People were always looking over at our table and children would be giggling. Often I found it extremely embarrassing.

'Why do you do this, Derek?' I would ask. He answered

simply, 'It's to give me more time.' That was the subject closed, as far as he was concerned, and the end of the matter. That is until the next alarm clock went off and the whole scene was re-enacted. This always made us laugh. Was anyone else in the world having this experience, or even a similar one? It was surreal.

Along with Derek's childlike innocence and simplicity went some amazing extraordinary abilities. He had talents most people could not understand, and his memory was phenomenal. For example, Derek would meet someone, ask their name and where they were from. A year or even several years later, if he met that same person again, he could remember their name and where they were from. He was always accurate. If he asked your date of birth, within minutes he could tell you the actual day of your birth. On checking this out later, he was always right. He could also tell you what day your birthday would fall on many years in to the future. On checking this information laboriously with pen and paper, it was found to be accurate every time. Derek could take his mind in to the past a century or two and name events and dates with the accuracy of a history book. Similarly he could project his mind in to the future and predict dates of forthcoming events. Whenever Derek visited the cinema he would read the credits when the film was over, then later that evening, or the next day, could repeat them with total accuracy.

On one occasion when Derek was visiting us in Belfast, he asked Dad to drive him to Ballyalton House, outside Newtownards, the place where he had happy childhood memories. When we got in to the car, Derek directed Dad from my house to the exact same road and found the house where he had not been for forty years. He was only four years old when he was last there, and yet he even remembered having his photograph taken in his little toy car outside the wall of Ballyalton House. To prove this to me, he asked Dad to photograph him standing with me at the same wall. When we were going through his things after he died, we found the two photographs together.

Family life was of the utmost importance to Derek. He spent every birthday with me. His ritual was that on 9 September he would travel to Belfast early, and I would meet him and take him to the Stranmillis Road, to the house next door to the one where we had lived as children. This

Revisiting the wall at Ballyalton, 1982, remembering happy childhood times

house was now a restaurant, and first we would have tea, complete with the funny stories and alarm clocks going off. At lunchtime Derek would ask the waiters and waitresses their names and where they were from, then he would introduce himself: 'I'm Derek and I'm from Dublin. This is my sister Helen and she's from Belfast. What's your name and where are you from?' Exactly a year later we would go back to the same restaurant, as Derek did not like change. On entering the door, Derek would remember everyone's name, where they were from, and even asked about the staff that were off that day. Time spent with Derek was certainly different. After lunch we always walked through Botanic Gardens as he liked to sit amongst the trees and look at the ever-changing leaves, where he found comfort as a little boy in the summertimes of his childhood.

Another amazing ability of Derek's was that on entering a building of any size, he would look around briefly and, after a short time, could tell with amazing accuracy the exact number of windows the building had. On counting the windows slowly, he was always right. How on earth was this possible? No one could understand it.

Derek had his own unique views on death. He believed

that the life of man was similar to the leaves on a tree. Each leaf was unique but had exactly the same life cycle as all the other leaves. Each began as a tiny bud, later unfolded in to a tiny, fresh green leaf in springtime, and in the fullness of summer reached its peak of beauty as it decorated the tree. Autumn came, the leaf began to change, and although it lost its colour of summer, it developed a richer, even more beautiful colour. When winter finally arrived, the leaf would shrivel up and simply be blown off the tree by the winds. If you looked really carefully where the leaf had lived its individual life on the tree, you could see another tiny bud waiting for springtime, when the whole cycle would repeat itself. Throughout all this activity, the tree itself, although giving life to the individual leaf, would stand, remaining unaffected. Were we not all the same?

Derek often assured me that Dublin City Council was going to build a statue of him and erect it in O'Connell Street after he had gone. 'How do you know, Derek? Why would they build a statue of you?' I asked. He always replied in the same way: 'Of course they'll put up a statue of me in O'Connell Street, didn't they build a statue of Molly Malone? She didn't even work for the council! I've worked for them for years and haven't even missed a day. If they built a statue of her then they'll definitely build a statue of me. Then I will be seen on the streets of Dublin for ever.' He smiled fondly at the thought of this.

Whenever anyone we knew died, Derek always wanted to know the date and time of the event, which interested him more than the emotion of the occasion. I thought he may react somewhat differently if it were a close family member who died, but he did not. When Dad died suddenly, I wrote to Derek to prepare him. When I saw Derek in person again he wanted the details of the time and date and what colour Dad was wearing. He then added, 'Well, I'm glad it happened in front of you and not me, for it would have spoiled my day.'

Some of Derek's work colleagues in the depot planted an evergreen tree and erected a plaque beside it in memory of Dad. This was a kind gesture and Derek often took us to see this tree. He asked for some clothing of Dad's and would put the cloth under his shirt and sit looking at the tree. It made him feel close to Dad, rather like a child with his or her comfort blanket.

Several years later, when Mum died, Derek was again more interested in the date and time of the occasion than his feelings about it. He then repeated his familiar catchphrase: 'I'm glad it happened it front of you and not me for it would have spoiled my day.' All I could do was laugh and hug him. He added, 'Mammy is *not* going to have an evergreen tree planted in her memory because she doesn't like green and anyone who doesn't like the colour green cannot be given an evergreen tree.' That was the subject closed for him.

Hopefully he was spared the grief and sorrow that accompany the death of a family member which most of us experience. Derek did not mind anyone dying, just as long as it was not anywhere near him to spoil his day.

CHAPTER SIX
THE IMPORTANT ROLE OF CHURCH

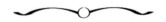

CHURCH ALWAYS FEATURED strongly in Derek's life. When we were young children, in the 1940s and 1950s, absolutely everyone went to church. There was nothing else to do on a Sunday. Children were forbidden to play outside, and all playgrounds were kept locked. Picture houses and shops were also closed, except the newsagents who only opened for a short time on a Sunday morning to enable those more daring members of society to buy a Sunday paper. It was considered by many people to be a sin to read a Sunday paper on Sunday. Most of those people kept their paper in a safe drawer or cupboard and read it during the week.

On Sunday mornings, everyone capable of walking dressed up in their one good outfit and, en masse, walked down the Stranmillis Road, to attend their various places of worship around the area. If you were not seen to be attending church everyone wanted to know why. The good outfits reserved for Sundays were usually removed after church and put away carefully until the following Sunday – that is unless you were visiting relatives or had relatives or friends coming to visit you. If there was a wedding, or any other special occasion, then that one good outfit would be brought out with care, and worn. Many men put moth balls around their one good suit, hoping to ward off moths. The smell of camphor in these moth balls was quite pungent – no wonder the moths stayed out of their wardrobes.

During the week most people wore basic, unattractive clothing, whatever the rationing allowed. Most areas had a good dressmaker, a gifted woman who was expert at sewing. The local women would buy cloth, give it to the dressmaker and have an outfit made up; that is how most of us got our clothes.

Sunday afternoons were for Sunday school, and Sunday evenings were, again, for church. We usually attended in the morning and afternoon only. That was definitely enough!

As children, we felt church services were strict and disciplined. Everyone was deadly silent. If you opened your mouth at all, it was only to say a prayer or sing a hymn.

Laughter was absolutely forbidden. As a child I laughed a lot and was always in trouble for it.

I used to look around at the long gloomy faces and think to myself – if this is what heaven is like then I definitely do not want to go there. Derek and I just wanted to have fun, like the rest of the local children.

Derek needed the routine of church and never missed it. He liked the predictable ritual and especially the hymns, which, with his amazing brain, he could remember off by heart, having read them just once. He could also memorise the number of each hymn without having to look at the book. He amazed his minister, who probably would have had difficulty doing this himself. Derek found that most of the people, when in the church, were a bit nicer and friendlier towards him, therefore people who went to church were Goodies. I was always grateful that Derek found comfort in church, as this had helped him feel some sense of family and belonging throughout his many harsh experiences in life. Derek liked churches and went around them all. He took communion everywhere it was on offer. 'Why not?' he would say. 'Aren't we all the same? It doesn't matter where you are given it.'

The friendliest and happiest place of worship for Derek was Findlaters, also known as Abbey Presbyterian Church, in Dublin. Although he lived nowhere near Abbey, Derek would set one of his many alarm clocks really early, get up and make the journey from the other side of Dublin. He would wait for a bus, walk to another bus stop and get a second bus, then have yet another walk to reach Abbey Church. To Derek, it was worth it. He loved his ritual, and received a warm welcome; it was the nearest he could get to the family life he craved in Dublin.

After church he had lunch at the Kingfisher, then made the same journey back to the other side of the city. Whenever we spent the weekend with him, he insisted we follow the same routine, which, of course, we did. I hoped some of these kind people, Goodies to Derek, would understand his vulnerability and keep an eye on him, making sure he was all right.

Later on in Derek's life, when I was desperately trying to find safe accommodation for him, Abbey Church proved invaluable by giving me addresses and contact numbers of possible places for Derek to stay, both short- and long-term, in the event of him being made homeless for any reason.

This was also a lovely link of friendship to our family, and Derek was always pleased if we got up early on a Sunday morning and travelled to meet him in his church. He would introduce us to absolutely everyone and make sure we felt as 'at home' as he did.

CHAPTER SEVEN
THE DIAGNOSIS

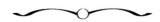

EREK WAS A UNIQUE, special, and complex character. A combination of a vulnerable, innocent young child, filled with trust and love towards everyone, and also a man with extraordinary mental ability beyond the range of most people. I often wondered if there was anyone else besides myself who could understand this. Was he unique, or did he have some mental condition which the world misunderstood?

I asked my own doctor and many other doctors and medical professionals for help. I was always given the same answer: Derek would first need to visit a GP, who would then refer him to a psychiatrist to be assessed. Sadly there was no way under the sun that I could persuade Derek to undergo this. After all, he was well and happy; for him life was good, and whenever anyone enquired after his health, he always said the same thing: 'I'm grand.'

Around this period I became aware of an Austrian

philosopher named Rudolf Steiner. Steiner was a man of exceptional spiritual knowledge and compassion. Due to his teachings and influence, many villages were set up in rural areas to look after adults similar to Derek. If only I could get Derek placed in one of these communities known as Camphill Communities, then Derek would, at last, be properly cared for. He would be given nutritious cooked food, have clean clothes, and the sense of family which he craved throughout his life in Dublin. In return, Derek could work on the land and with the animals. Derek was always a conscientious hard worker, and followed instructions to the letter.

I made contact with these people, both in the north and the Republic of Ireland, went to investigate the communities and found the people most helpful. The set-up seemed perfect and tailor-made for Derek. The only problem was Derek himself: would he be prepared to live there? He had been used to his freedom on the streets of Dublin, which was his home, and had his own 'space', even though his rents were unaffordable.

I broached the subject with him, he listened carefully, thought about it, and said firmly: 'No, I like my freedom and my own money.' As an adult, it was entirely his decision, and

I had to accept this. I also contacted Dublin City Council, who employed Derek, and was told that in order to get Derek a council flat, he would need the recommendation of a housing officer and a medical diagnosis.

Eventually I arranged to meet with a housing officer from the council, and showed him Derek's awful room. He agreed that Derek did, indeed, need a council flat, and he was put on the list. He also advised me to contact a local councillor and put Derek's case to him or her, as hopefully this would carry some weight in helping things along.

I was given a list of councillors and chose a woman, hoping she would have compassion for his plight on hearing his story. I was lucky. Councillor Mary Freehill spent time listening to me telling her a little bit about Derek's life and how I was worried about his future if he could no longer work. He would not be in a position to pay his ever-increasing rent, and my fear was of him becoming homeless on the streets of Dublin.

Around this time I became friendly with a psychiatric nurse who lent me some papers on a condition only recently discovered called Asperger's Syndrome. According to his experience, Derek appeared to have all the classic symptoms of the condition.

As I read carefully through these medical papers, I was seeing an exact mirror image of my brother. He did indeed have Asperger's Syndrome. The poor man had gone through his entire life being totally misunderstood and seriously neglected. It was heartbreaking for me. At least I now knew what I was dealing with. At long last.

The next hurdle was to obtain an official medical letter for the council, to prove that Derek was vulnerable and needed secure accommodation. Eventually, after much persuasion, Derek reluctantly agreed to see a doctor as long as I went with him. After all, he was 'grand', so why on earth would he visit a doctor?

I slipped in to the doctor's surgery first and told her briefly that I desperately needed a letter from her, confirming that Derek had a mental condition which meant he needed safe, sheltered accommodation, and also that it had to be in Upper Rathmines, where Derek felt safe. (The Goodies lived in Upper Rathmines.)

When Derek was called in to the surgery, the doctor immediately understood him. He approached her with great enthusiasm and said, 'Hello, what's your name?'

'My name is Ciara,' she answered.

'How are you doing, Ciara? Where are you from? My name's Derek and I'm from Dublin. This is my sister Helen and she's from Belfast.'

'How is your health, Derek?' the doctor asked.

'I'm grand, Ciara,' he replied, 'simply grand.' Then he added, 'And how's your health, Ciara?'

Then he sat down happily with the doctor for a bit of craic. After all, wasn't she a nice lady, and what else do you do when you're sitting down with someone? The doctor and I exchanged knowing glances and simply had to laugh. Derek got the letter he so desperately needed to enable him to get a safe home for his senior years.

I could soon rest easy knowing that Derek would end his days in an area of Dublin he knew and loved.

Chapter Eight
The Senior Years

BEFORE DEREK WAS rehoused, an unfortunate event occurred which brought the urgency of his situation home to me forcefully. Stan and I had arranged to meet Derek, but he did not turn up. We made our way to his house, and down to the tiny basement where he was living.

When we knocked on his door there was no answer. We kept calling his name, and eventually he answered: 'Who is it, who is it?'

'It's me, Helen. You arranged to meet us. Open the door,' I said.

He seemed reluctant to do this. After some persuasion, we heard furniture being moved around, then he opened his door just a crack and peeped out. His door was barricaded up.

He was obviously afraid and simply would not come out or talk about the situation. We had to leave him there, and when he closed his door we could hear him putting the furniture back and shutting himself in again.

We knocked on another tenant's door to try and find out what had happened. Apparently a gang of men had smashed in the front door and broken in to the rooms in the house, obviously looking for money or anything valuable. The other tenants had reported the incident to the Garda – they knew it was most likely an isolated event, and simply got on with their lives – but poor Derek was left shaken and frightened and feeling alone again in what appeared to be an alien world.

My thoughts drifted back to his earlier years when he was barricaded in his little back-attic room to keep him safe and also to hide him away from the world. Now, fifty years later, here he was again, barricaded in a tiny basement room, hiding from the Baddies who were now in Lower Rathmines.

However, Derek also encountered many acts of kindness and generosity on the streets of Dublin. One particular incident always moves me. On a bitterly cold winter day, Derek was walking past a synagogue, just as a man happened to be coming out. When he saw Derek in the cold, he took off his fur-lined wool overcoat, put it around Derek's shoulders and fastened it on him. 'Keep it,' he smiled to Derek, then hurried away in to the snow before Derek had time to thank him properly. Never in my life have I heard of such a loving act. The coat was beautifully made and obviously expensive, yet the owner did not want any reward or even recognition for the kindness he had shown to a complete stranger.

When Derek grew older, his long dark beard turned pure white, and he put on a lot of weight. Due to his appearance and love of little children, he was often asked to act as Santa Claus at Christmas time. This role was perfect – all he needed was the red coat and he was indeed Santa Claus. This pleased him a lot.

On Derek's sixtieth birthday – which was on 9/9/1999, the number he loved and talked about – he came to see me in Belfast, as always, to follow our familiar routine. When I saw him getting off the coach I was shocked at the sudden change in his physical appearance. His back was bent over and he was walking really slowly.

'Are you all right?' I asked. 'Have you a sore back?'

The answer was the same as always: 'I'm grand, Helen, simply grand.' Derek was always grand. As on other birthdays, he remembered all the staff in our usual restaurant, everyone's name and where they came from; he even remembered the names of some who had since left to work elsewhere.

The birthday lunch was predictable and as hilarious as

always. The staff knew what was coming, but members of the wider public did not: the same stories, the password for getting past a goose, and his various alarm clocks going off, then being stopped and reset.

When we took our usual walk through Botanic Gardens, I noticed he had become unbelievably slow. Derek's strength and natural good health were deteriorating. Years of poor nutrition, working out-of-doors in all weather conditions, and his squalid housing conditions were taking their toll. In Derek's mind he was really happy and always 'grand'.

Derek asked the council for easier work, and they gave him the job of keeping the parks tidy. One of his duties was to sweep up the autumn leaves. This was the ideal type of work for him, with his affinity with leaves and trees, which, after all, were no different from the life cycle of people. Derek enjoyed the company of the people coming through the parks, and especially the children who played there. He knew everyone by name. He jogged along like this for the next few years.

In 2000 Derek was finally allocated a ground floor flat in Upper Rathmines, his favourite place to live. The weekend

Sunday lunch at the Kingfisher, 2006, one of Derek's rituals

Derek's sixty-seventh birthday in hospital, September 2006

Stan and I moved him in was one of joyful celebration. Stan hired a large van and spent the whole weekend settling him in. Derek was having trouble with his legs and I eventually persuaded him to see a doctor. He was taken in to St James Hospital, where he stayed and was looked after for a week. The staff got to know him, and he was issued with a medical card. At long last Derek was in the system.

Every week Derek attended St James Hospital, and on his last birthday the nurses presented him with a cake and candles as they sang Happy Birthday to him. He thoroughly enjoyed this and had his photograph taken with the nurses. Where in the world except Ireland would such a thing happen?

Derek finally retired from work at the age of sixty-four. He had worked for Dublin City Council for thirty-four years without ever having taken a day off. The Council presented him with a beautiful large certificate in recognition of his years of loyal, unbroken service, and a book on Dublin City, also inscribed, thanking him for his years of loyalty and hard work.

Our monthly visits to spend time with Derek continued and had become a pleasant routine in our lives.

Cathair Bhaile Átha Cliath
City of Dublin

Presented to
Derek Rowe
Parks and Landscape Services
In appreciation of
34 Years of Loyal Service
to
Dublin City Parks
and the
Citizens of Dublin

Dublin City Manager

Date 28th February 2003

The certificate awarded to Derek for his loyal service to Dublin City Council

CHAPTER NINE
THE FINAL PARTING

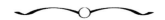

THE LAST TIME we saw Derek alive was Christmas 2006. After church we had our usual lunch at the Kingfisher and exchanged gifts. When we dropped him home to Upper Rathmines, he leaned out of his green-painted front door, as he had done for the past six years, and said the same thing as always: 'Goodbye, good luck. When will you be back?'

'We'll be back to see you the first weekend in February, Derek,' I answered.

'I'll write to you and send you your birthday card two weeks early in case of a postal strike,' he added.

We embraced, and I kissed his soft bearded cheek.

'Goodbye now, good luck, good luck.' He stood at his door waving to us until we were out of sight.

Michael, my son, and I received letters from him in January. Two weeks before my birthday Derek's card did not arrive. This had never happened before. I hoped he was all right. I knew we would be seeing him at the weekend anyway, so I tried not to worry too much. Derek never used a phone; he did not like phones and preferred letter-writing. His flat did not have a phone.

The following afternoon, the last weekend in January, I got the phone call I had always been dreading: Derek had not been seen for a couple of weeks. Had he been in contact with me? Apparently he had missed two church services and also missed two hospital appointments. This was totally out of character. Derek needed his set routines. Something must be wrong. My peaceful afternoon was shattered as I felt the panic rising within me.

The Garda were called and they broke in to his flat. I waited for an hour to hear the news. That hour was the longest in my life. Roisin, the warden, phoned me and said, 'I'm afraid it's the worst possible news. Derek has been found dead inside his flat. I'm so sorry. He was really popular with the neighbours here – everyone liked him.'

All I could do was stand and cry. Derek had been in my life from the day I was born in our Stranmillis home. He had been with me longer than any other person and now he was gone.

The warden and Garda were extremely kind and helpful. I was advised to travel to Dublin as soon as possible. They organised everything, which spared our family much heartache.

We did indeed travel to Dublin again, that first weekend in February as promised, to visit Derek, only, sadly, it was for his funeral. Two car-loads of our now grown-up family drove from Belfast, all of us hurting. As I walked towards Derek's coffin, I thought of what he would have said if our roles had been reversed: 'I don't mind anyone dying, as long as they don't do it anywhere near me, for it would spoil my day.'

Derek, you definitely spoiled my day.

This parting was more painful than any other parting in my life. Derek was more than my brother. He had become my child, my friend, my pen pal, the person I lunched with in Dublin and a special soulmate whom nobody else fully understood.

On our arrival at Abbey Church, we were overwhelmed by the crowd of people who had come to pay their last respects. I thought it might only be our immediate family and a few church members. No, people from every walk of life were there: church members, young and old, representatives from

Dublin City Council and Derek's former workmates from the depot. His neighbours from Rathmines all came, too. They had organised a Mass for him in Rathmines Roman Catholic Chapel where he sometimes worshipped. From there they had travelled to Abbey Church for his other service.

What a send-off. He deserved it. He was a man who loved everyone without exception, and I hoped that at some level he now knew that they also loved him.

Reverend Alan Boal gave a most uplifting service in celebration of Derek's life. He described Derek as a special, gentle and unique person. He read Keats' poem called 'Autumn Leaves', as it reminded him of Derek, who never tired of sweeping up the autumn leaves. To Derek, the leaves were also his friends, all part of the one life we all share together.

The final part of his journey was from the church to Glasnevin Crematorium with only our immediate family. This completed the ceremony, and Derek, my very special brother, went off with the beautiful flowers he had been given, his Rosary round his hands and a picture of Jesus on his heart. We had found this picture with his personal belongings and thought he would like to have it close to him.

Sitting in the Gresham Hotel after Derek's funeral, I was pleased that we had all decided to wear something green in his memory. The beautiful, haunting music of 'The Sally Gardens' was playing softly in the background. I felt my throat tightening with emotion as I listened. 'The Sally Gardens' was the first music Derek heard when he was born. Mum used to sing it to him as she tenderly cradled him in her arms. Now, on the day of his funeral, it was being played again.

There was another strange occurrence. When the meal was over the waiter handed me the bill, which came to exactly 108 euros: nine times twelve, Derek's favourite number. It was as though Derek was there with us all. It was exactly how he would have chosen it. He would have loved to see us all wearing green, delighted to hear 'The Sally Gardens' being played and, if the number nine had featured in the bill, he would have given it a mention.

Perhaps some time in the future someone *will* decide to erect a statue in Derek's memory. For now, every time I see the changing leaves in the parks of Dublin and Belfast, I will always think of him standing among them, smiling at me.

My dearest memory of Derek, close to his beloved trees

Derek's ashes are scattered in the Garden of Remembrance at Glasnevin. He had successfully fulfilled his life's ambition, which was to spend his days around the trees in the outdoors, and work, live and end his life in Dublin city.

He died safely in the comfort of his own home in Upper Rathmines. He never had to go in to an institution or grow old in a home. Nor did he have to lie suffering in a hospital bed. He had his space, his freedom and his dignity right until his last moment here.

Against all the odds, Derek's colourful life had been successful. He coped alone, and was happy. What he was able to achieve shows what is possible. He touched the lives of hundreds of people on the streets of Dublin. Derek was loved, and he will never be forgotten.

My Personal Tribute to Derek

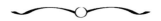

D EREK, YOU HAVE touched me in a deeper place than I ever thought possible.

You were a unique soul, a special being who showed our world the importance of finding happiness and joy in the simplest things of life. The joy of the sun rising each morning. The pleasure of hearing the birds sing. Your love of all nature and animals. The great enthusiasm you showed when another person caught your eye or smiled at you. The pleasure you felt in watching the seasons change, and your awesome wonder at the colourful, ever-changing beauty of the leaves on the trees.

You greeted each person and each situation as new, showing us the importance of living life fully in the present moment.

I am privileged to have been your sister. May your soul rest in the peace of eternity.

Helen

Printed in the United Kingdom
by Lightning Source UK Ltd.
129001UK00001B/46-66/P